I Don't Feel Called
(Thank the Lord!)

Don W. Hillis

Tyndale House Publishers
Wheaton, Illinois

Coverdale House Publishers Ltd.
London, England

Acknowledgment

The author expresses sincere appreciation
to artist Dave Harbaugh for the privilege of
using the cartoons found herein. He also
extends his gratitude to *Moody Monthly*,
*The King's Business, Evangelical Action,
Scripture Press Youth Quarterly, World
Vision*, and the *Good News Broadcaster*,
for permission to reprint the chapters that
originally appeared as articles in
those magazines.

Library of Congress Catalog Card Number 72-97651
ISBN 8423-1570-5

Contents

How do you relate
opportunity
to responsibility?
If this book
opens your eyes
to more opportunities,
then what?

What! Missions is exciting?

Sure it is! Anything Jesus Christ
does is exciting to the man who
has eyes to see him and
heart to love him.

The most challenging period of
church history was not fifty
years ago or five centuries ago.
It was not even yesterday.
It is today.

Less than 200 years ago, foreign
missions appeared to be a
forgotten cause with missionaries
few and far between. Today,
30,000 Protestant missionaries

from the United States serve Christ in more than a hundred countries of the world; and most of this tremendous growth has taken place in the last fifty years.

Why, the sheer magnitude of missions is exciting. In his omniscience, God has opened the floodgates of technological advance on the twentieth century. Scientific and technological progress is enabling the church in this hour to accomplish what no church of any previous century could have ever done. Because world population has more than tripled in the last 100 years, it has become absolutely necessary for the missionary program to possess mass evangelism and Bible-teaching media; and God has given them to us.

Great commercial airlines are whisking missionaries today from one end of the world to the other in a matter of a couple of days. A trip that took William Carey three months to make now takes a few hours. Automobiles and small planes have taken the place of the ox cart on foreign fields, and servants of Christ are getting to more cities and villages with the Good News than ever before. The missionary now possesses tools which make it possible for him to reach more people in one week than Paul reached in a lifetime. This is missions' greatest hour!

This is not to underestimate the quality of Paul's ministry or of any other servant of

God who has labored, fulfilling the Great Commission. We need more men of that quality, and we appreciate the tremendous contribution missionaries of the past have made, not only to the lives of individuals but to entire societies and nations.

Today's missionary program has the privilege of building on this fact. Some nations are open today because their people are aware of the benefits brought to their culture by the foreign missionary and his Christian message.

Think of the countries that have thrown their doors open to Christian radio broadcasting. Radio stations all over the world are selling choice time to gospel broadcasters. Think of the tremendous outreach of those radio ministries. At the turn of the century, there was no World Radio Missionary Fellowship with its great outreach from Latin America. Before World War II, there was no Far East Broadcasting Company with its hundreds of hours of gospel broadcasting blanketing the Orient every month. Thirty years ago, there was no Trans World Radio with its immense transmitter power dedicated to the gospel; there was no HLKX, no TIFC, and no ELWA.

Though Bible societies and other Christian literature organizations were operating before the turn of this century, it has been during the last twenty-five years that they have taken their greatest step forward.

Christian printing and publishing programs are running at full steam in their efforts to keep ahead of demands for gospel literature in the vernacular languages. Every year the production and distribution of Christian literature exceeds the previous year. This is indeed missions' greatest hour!

It would be difficult to estimate the contribution the church of Jesus Christ has made in the realm of adult literacy and education on many mission fields. Millions have been taught to read and write, while additional millions have gone through mission-directed grade schools, high schools, and colleges. In no other century has so much suffering been relieved in the name of the Great Physician as in this one. Thousands of mission hospitals, leprosariums, tuberculosis sanitariums, and orphanages are ministering to needy people around the world with a God-given compassion for the bodies and souls of men.

Things are happening today even in the home office administration of missionary programs. There is increased efficiency. This speaks well for the work. The accounting departments of most foreign mission societies are administered by well-trained accounting personnel. In some cases, computing machines are adding to the efficiency. The travel and visa arrangements are handled by men and women who are experienced in dealing with foreign governments, travel agencies, and shipping companies. Candidate selection is carried on by men of God who know how to screen applicants and to counsel them about their preparation for the foreign field. Home office administration is combining a wholesome spiritual concern for world evangelization and a quiet efficiency which carries a load the supporting churches could never bear.

Never in all history has a nation been so uniquely qualified to carry an overwhelming share of the program of world evangelism as the United States. In a special way God has preserved and blessed our nation in order to make this true. Though America has had its share of internal and international conflicts, yet God has saved it from the devastation and economic destruction so many other countries have suffered.

No country has ever had the economic wealth or the Christian manpower to plow into world evangelism that America enjoys. God has entrusted to this great country one-half of the world's wealth, even though her people make up less than one-sixteenth of the world's population. Furthermore, there are more boys and girls, men and women in Sunday schools in America on any given Sunday than in all other countries of the world put together. What a source of manpower!

America has more than 60,000 Christian young people in Bible institutes and Bible colleges. Thousands of others are in our Christian liberal arts colleges and on State university campuses. Never in any nation has such a source of potential missionary personnel been available to the Lord of the Harvest. Though the number of new missionaries annually going to the foreign fields of the world falls short of the need, yet it surpasses those who went out during any other century of missionary history.

It is also noteworthy that the last fifty years have given us more missionary societies ministering in more countries in more ways and through more media than ever before. There is no gift, aptitude, or legitimate educational background that a young person cannot exploit for the glory of God today in some mission field under some mission board. Mission societies are growing in number and size. Most of them are pleading for help. This bears optimistic testimony to the fact that they believe these are days of great opportunities.

More and more nations allow the use of Bible-teaching as a part of the weekly school curriculum. High schools and university campuses in scores of nations are open to teen teams and gospel films. Space can be bought to advertise the gospel in the large secular newspapers of the world's cities.

Even television time is available for a price.

Who says all of this opportunity doesn't suggest responsibility? And how can life really be meaningful except as it relates to God's program of reaching the world for Christ?

> And when they heard the roaring in the sky above the house, crowds came running to see what it was all about, and were stunned to hear their own languages being spoken by the disciples.

> "How can this be?" they exclaimed. "For these men are all from Galilee; and yet we hear them speaking all the native languages of the lands where we were born!"
> Acts 2:6-8/*The Living Bible*

IS THERE SOMEONE YOU'D LIKE TO HELP OVERSEAS?
YEAH,... MY CHEMISTRY PROF...
GUARD

Missions is
not a response
to man's desire
for God,
but to God's desire
for man.

What!
God loves
people?

Of course he does. But would
you believe it is possible to
serve the Lord without knowing
that he loves people? I know.
I've done it, and maybe my
experience will be helpful to you.

You can be sure I had
memorized John 3:16 long
before I went as a missionary
to India. But it is one thing to
be able to quote a verse; it is
another to have it operative in
the heart. And somehow the
English translation of that verse
is pretty impersonal. If it had
only been translated, "For God

so loved *people* . . .," it might have helped.

I wasn't long in India before I found myself "turning off" when I came in contact with saffron-robed Hindu priests. After all, they represented all that was false and anti-Christ in Hinduism. So I transferred my hatred for the false teachings to the people who promulgated them. I made no attempt to proclaim the love of God to the Hindu priests I met. I had not really learned that God loves people.

Returning to the States, I did the same thing with the followers of false religious systems and cults. I found it easy to slam the door in the face of Mormons, Jehovah's Witnesses, and Christian Scientists. It was difficult to be anything but cold and indifferent to Catholic priests and nuns. I made no serious attempt to share the grace of Christ with any of them. I had not learned that God loves people.

The New Testament indicates that this was a common disease in the days of Christ. The Pharisees (the conservatives of Judaism) were deeply infected with it. They sat in judgment on Jesus for eating with sinners. It was Simon the Pharisee who piously assured himself that Jesus could not be a prophet and at the same time accept the worship of a sinful but repentant woman. The scribes and Pharisees could not understand why Jesus would stoop to the level of going to the home of Zacchaeus for a meal. They had not learned that God loves people.

The Jews in general held within their hearts a smoldering hatred for Samaritans. They saw them as religious mongrels whom God himself could never love. This in part led Jesus to tell the story of the Good Samaritan, though he knew his hearers would have much preferred a story of a good Jew.

Unfortunately, the Lord's disciples were not free from this foul disease. They were amazed that Jesus would waste his time and risk his reputation to talk to a woman—to a Samaritan woman—and to one of unsavory reputation at that.

The "beloved disciple," John, and his brother, James, shared in this hatred of Samaritans. Remember their words concerning a certain Samaritan village?

> "Lord, wilt thou that we command fire to come down from heaven, and consume them . . .?" (Luke 9:45).

In response Jesus pointedly informed them that they didn't really understand that God loves people.

It is doubtful that the disciples comprehended God's love for the world even after Pentecost. They responded positively to the Lord's command for them to be witnesses in

Jerusalem and Judaea. But they "turned off" when he added Samaria and the uttermost part of the earth. Nothing short of persecution could drive the early Jewish believers to share the love of God with the Gentiles.

Perhaps Peter was the slowest to learn the lesson. As it is with some of the rest of us who talk about God's love, there was an immense difference between Peter's world and God's world. Peter found it difficult to believe that God could love people outside of his own little world. Love the Jews? Of course. Love the Gentiles? Horrors, no!

The tenth chapter of Acts unveils God's patient dealing with Peter in regard to this deep-seated flaw. Peter, who loved God too much to eat anything unclean, knew God too little to comprehend his love. The conversion of Cornelius and his household became a life-changing experience for Peter. He saw the same blessed Spirit through whom many had been convicted of sin, righteousness, and judgment at Pentecost, bring salvation into a Gentile home. He learned once and for all that God loves people.

All of this raises the question, "Who turns you off?" Is it the beggar, the alcoholic, the hippie, the cultist, the black man, the next door neighbor, or someone who owes you money? If anyone turns you off, perhaps, like Peter, you have something more to learn about the dimensions of God's love.

I'm glad I can say things have changed. I no longer judge a man by his clerical garb or religious trappings. I reject his errors, but I accept him. Like Saul before his conversion, he may be closer to the kingdom than I realize. Every man, regardless of color, dress, culture, language, education, economic standard, or religion is a potential believer. If he is ever to learn that God loves him, it will have to be through people like you and me who have learned that God loves people.

The fact is, we are to be witnesses, not basically because men are lost but because God is love. Missions springs primarily from the deep soil of God's character, not from the lost condition of men. We are soul winners not because men are unrighteous, but because God is gracious.

This is another way of saying that man's salvation is not the first meaning of Calvary. Its deeper message is God's vindication. At the cross God vindicated his holy character while voicing his love for unholy creatures.

With the fall of man in Eden, the omnipotent One was robbed of his richest treasure. From the finite aspect God was no longer God, for Satan had won his point and had become the "god of this world." Man was then "without God." What was worse, God was without man. Adam and Eve had become slaves to another sovereign and servants in a kingdom destined to destruction.

In the eternal councils of God stands the Cross, destined to fit into the framework of time. The divine Architect had included the making of a rough piece of wood upon which he himself would die. Because he is "The Lamb slain from the foundation of the world," that cross fits into any period in the history of man. Its shadow is seen repeatedly throughout the Old Testament. One is left with the impression that the cross could have been erected at the point where God revealed Genesis 3:15 to Adam; or it could have been erected at the Passover or in the soil of Palestine, while Isaiah wrote the 53rd chapter of his book, "He was wounded for our transgressions. . . ."

From an eternal perspective the battle tide was always in favor of the kingdom of God. It was not, however, until the crucifixion and resurrection that this became historically evident. It was there Christ became sin for us that we might become the righteousness of God in him. At Calvary men became available to God. Sinful men are now savable, lost men findable, bound men freeable, and dead men livable.

The missionary's task is to bring men to God from idols, to the Savior from Satan, to life from death. Note the order. The soul winner's most meaningful motivation is not to deliver men from something, but to Someone. The

missionary is not basically constrained to
lift men out of darkness, but to bring them
to the Light. It is life, not death; heaven,
not hell that makes witnessing important.
It is not hatred for Satan, but love for God
that makes a true missionary.

God exists that man may enjoy him, but man
was created for God to enjoy. Man is God's
richest treasure and must be restored to him,
not only for the sake of the treasure but for
the sake of the Owner.

We preach not so much because men need
God but because God wants men. We go
forth with the gospel not so much because
men are godless but because God is manless.
Salvation has been provided, not just that
men might rejoice in heaven, but that heaven
might rejoice in men.

Though the arms of the Cross reach around
the world as an expression of man's
opportunity for deliverance from sin, we
do not fully understand Calvary until we
have seen it from above. From that perspective
we begin to realize that missions is not a
response to man's desire for God, but to God's
desire for man. The Great Commission was
his thought, not ours. It grew out of his desire
to enjoy eternal fellowship with men. For
his sake, then, let's get on with the job. Let's
demonstrate the fact that God loves people.

> God showed how much he loved
> us by sending his only Son into

this wicked world to bring to
us eternal life through his death.
In this act we see what real
love is: it is not our love for God,
but his love for us when he
sent his Son to satisfy God's
anger against our sins.
1 John 4:9, 10/*TLB*

There is something
meaningful and
stabilizing
about knowing
you have been
conscripted by God
for his service.

 # What!
I'm drafted?

A loud cheer rang out from the small group huddled tightly around a flagpole. A young man who had contributed little toward whatever the American flag might stand for had just burned his draft card. America probably saw more draft card burners and dodgers during the Viet Nam war than any other nation would have tolerated. That particular brand of irresponsibility was not, however, typical of the vast majority of America's youth.

Though Christianity in general

deplores deliberate and violent attempts to destroy governmental authority, it faces a far more serious situation within its own ranks. The church harbors hundreds of spiritual draft dodgers. They are those who have heard Christ say,

> "You have not chosen me,
> but I have chosen you and
> ordained you that you should
> go and bring forth fruit"

—but have declined to go. They are those who, knowing the demands of the Great Commission, have elected to bypass them. They have been chosen to be soldiers of Christ and ambassadors for God, but they have burned their "draft cards."

Perhaps missionary recruiting officers are more to blame for this than they are ready to admit. They have often failed to present the Lordship of Jesus Christ. They have placed Christian service on a human option level. They have probably left you with the impression that you can fight the Lord's battles if you desire; or you can opt for that which is less strenuous—perhaps paying an occasional tax to salve the conscience. Does the challenge the missionary presents look like a poor second to the opportunity the world offers? Then something is drastically wrong. Either the man who has presented missions has failed to communicate the real truth, or you as a listener have for some reason turned him off.

Apparently we need a new understanding of the fact that doing the will of God is not an option; it is an order.

Christ is sovereign, ruling over the nations, accomplishing his will and gathering out from among the nations "a people for his name." He is doing this through the instrumentality of soldiers who are drafted for his battles. The Scriptures indicate that the men and women God has used have not been volunteers; they have been draftees.

Noah

Noah was not a volunteer for that overwhelming task which saved the world and wrote his name indelibly in history. He was conscripted by God. He would never have accepted the job under any other circumstance. He labored for 120 years under divine compulsion.

Had Noah been a "volunteer," the apparent insanity of the project he was undertaking would have caused him to give up long before the completion of the job. He had doubtless never heard of a flood. The concept of building a boat to hold birds and beasts must have seemed preposterous to him. Nothing short of implicit faith in the word of God and total obedience to the will of God could have bound Noah to the task given him. Noah was God's draftee, and he knew it.

Joseph

Joseph was drafted to be the "savior" of
Israel. The blueprint of his experiences was
not planned by him or by his parents. He
could not possibly have harmonized his
experiences in the pit, in Potiphar's house,
and in Pharaoh's prison with the dream of
supremacy God had given him in his early
teens. He had not gone to Egypt in response
to some missionary promotional program.
Somehow he had a faith that believed God
would fulfill his will in giving him that
promised place of leadership regardless of the
contrary winds of circumstances. Joseph
was not a volunteer; he was a draftee. He
bears testimony to this in his words,

> "Now therefore be not grieved,
> nor angry with yourselves, that
> ye sold me hither: for God did
> send me before you to preserve
> life" (Genesis 45:5).

Moses

It is difficult to know just when Moses first
felt God had selected him to deliver Israel
from Egypt. We know he had such a
conviction before the close of the first forty
years of his life. It was not until he was
eighty, however, that the Lord spoke to him
definitely about returning to Egypt as God's

selected general for delivering Israel.

Moses' excuses and persistent effort to avoid
becoming involved in such an assignment
are irrefutable proof that he was not a
volunteer. God overruled all of his excuses
and, as he went to face Pharaoh, he knew
he was going as a draftee of the God
of Abraham, Issac, and Jacob.

Jonah

No one would be tempted to suggest that
Jonah was a volunteer for a missionary
ministry in Ninevah. Apparently he was
willing to volunteer to preach and prophesy
to the people of Israel, but that's where his
volunteering terminated. His drastic but
futile efforts to avoid being conscripted into
the appointed task are too well known to
need reviewing. They simply stand as
irrefutable evidence that Jonah
was no volunteer.

Jeremiah

The prophet Jeremiah gives us a unique
testimony of assurance that he was God-
chosen. It was this very assurance that enabled
him to face years of difficult service for God.
He says the word of the Lord came to him,
saying,

> "Before I formed thee in the
> belly, I knew thee and before

thou camest forth out of the womb I sanctified thee; I have appointed thee a prophet unto the nations" (Jeremiah 1:5).

Though Jeremiah trembled before this assignment, God assured him that he would give him grace to "go to whomsoever I shall send thee" and power to speak "to whomsoever I shall command thee." To Jeremiah and to many other Old Testament prophets God had said, "You have not chosen me but I have chosen you."

The disciples

Who would suggest that Peter, James, John, and the other disciples were volunteers? Christ's command to them, "Follow me and I will make you to become fishers of men," was that of a recruiting officer.

Paul

And what about that belligerent Pharisee who was converted on the road to Damascus? He who said, "Woe is me if I preach not the gospel," knew he had been drafted by the King of all kings. He knew he was to be an apostle and an ambassador. Furthermore he gloried in it. It was the very assurance of his conscription that enabled him to labor more abundantly, to suffer more deeply, and to fight more faithfully.

You

The true servant of Jesus Christ is something more than a volunteer. He is one who is convinced that the option of how he should invest his life belongs to God. The missionary movement in the world today is looking for men and women to whom Christ's lordship is personally real. It is looking for men and women who are under the authority of the Lord of Harvest—for men and women who readily accept the Great Commission as an imperative to be obeyed.

Nothing enables a servant of Jesus Christ to be "steadfast, immovable, always abounding in the work of the Lord" as much as a deep conviction that he has been chosen by God for his service. There is something meaningful and stabilizing about knowing that you are a draftee.

> "You didn't choose me!
> I chose you! I appointed you
> to go and produce lovely fruit
> always, so that no matter what
> you ask for from the Father,
> using my name, he will give
> it to you."
> John 15:16/*TLB*

27

"I would like to be
a missionary,
but I turn off
when I think of
going from church
to church begging
for support."

What!
Raise my own
support?

"It is the complaint I hear with
more consistency than any
other," says Inter-Varsity's
David Howard. "Again and
again students say to me,
'I believe I am as committed to
the Lord as I can be. I want to
serve Jesus Christ. I am perfectly
willing to go overseas and serve
the Lord, but this business of
going around and drumming
up my support—I cannot buy it.
I will not buy it.'" Howard
describes the attitude of many
potential missionary candidates
in these words, "You've got

yourself set with all your affluence, and now I come to you on my hands and knees and ask you to support me."

Horace Fenton, Jr., general director of the Latin America Mission says, "If raising his own support by making contacts with churches and individuals 'bugs' a potential candidate today, we ought to be concerned about it. If our system is right, we ought to be able to prove it to these young people. If it's wrong, we ought to be seeking with them a better way to do the Lord's work."

Tom Watson, Jr., founder of Radio Station HLKX in Korea, adds, "They are right; it is a problem. There is something underlying the method that tends to degrade the candidate. It does support an economic double standard. The missionary does have experiences where he laughs because he doesn't want to cry. Maybe there is a better way; if so, what is it?"

Fortunately, it is possible to be both sympathetic toward the problem and also scriptural. And just as fortunately, the

Scriptures are far from silent on this issue.

There is no rebuttal to the fact that in the Old Testament economy those who served the Lord and his people (the priests, Levites, and prophets) lived off the tithes and offerings of the people. Furthermore, the Spirit of the Lord made strong pronouncement against his people whenever they were unfaithful in the matter of stewardship. There was a definite relationship between Israel's faithfulness in giving and God's blessings upon the nation. Both Haggai and Malachi said much about this.

But in case anyone objects to moving back into the Old Testament, we will move quickly into the New.

Jesus, who could have turned stones into bread and who did multiply loaves and fishes, lived off the gifts of his friends during his public ministry. Furthermore, he pulled the economic rug from under the feet of those he called into his service. He insisted that the fishermen should leave their fishing, the tax collector his tax collecting, and the tentmaker his tentmaking. And certainly we are no better than our Master or than his early servants.

When Jesus sent out the seventy "into every city and place," he commanded them to "carry neither purse, nor scrip, nor shoes." They were to accept the hospitality of those who would open their homes, "eating and drinking such things as they give: for the laborer is worthy of his hire" (Luke 10:4-7).

A study of the Epistles makes it plain that the servant of the Lord has a God-ordained *right to receive*. The ox that treads out the grain is not to be muzzled (1 Corinthians 9:9). The soldier is not to go to war at his own expense, and the farmer is expected to eat of the fruit of his labor (1 Corinthians 9:7).

Whether it involves the preacher in America or the missionary overseas, the Lord has ordained that those who "preach the gospel should live of the gospel" (1 Corinthians 9:14). And what is the basic difference between a pastor expecting his people to support him and an apostle (missionary) expecting churches to send him forth and support him?

As far as I can discover, Paul only once apologized to the Corinthian believers for anything. It involved his failure to insist that they should carry their share of his support. Furthermore, under the inspiration of the Holy Spirit, he gave them (and us) two full chapters of exhortation on the subject of Christian stewardship. He pled with the Corinthians to "abound in this grace also." He assured them that this is a way in which they could "prove the sincerity" of their love for God. He warned them of the danger of

sowing sparingly and encouraged them with
the reward of sowing bountifully. He assured
them that God is able to make all grace
abound toward them in this matter of
sacrificial giving. He reminded them that God
loves a cheerful giver.

As illustrations of true giving, Paul
used (1) the unselfishness of the Macedonian
believers who gave out of their deep poverty,
(2) the grace of liberality demonstrated
in the fact that Christ gave up the riches of
heaven and took upon himself earth's
poverty, (3) and the fact of the Father's
indescribable Gift to us.

Apparently Paul looked upon the Philippian
church as his "supporting church." To the
believers there he wrote,

> "I rejoice . . . that now at last
> your care of me has flourished
> again . . . ye have done well that
> ye did communicate with me
> (concerning giving and
> receiving) . . . not because I
> desire a gift; but I desire fruit
> that may abound to your
> account" (Philippians 4:10,
> 14, 17).

Ten of the last fourteen verses in this four-
chapter "circular letter" were written in
commendation of their financial assistance.

Though Paul as a missionary had learned how to be abased and how to abound, how to be full and how to hunger, he did not fail to rebuke those who were careless about giving to the Lord's servants or to commend those who were faithful. He felt it was his holy obligation to exhort believers to prove the sincerity of their love by supporting God's work.

The missionary of the Cross does not accept the gifts of God's people as handouts for his personal well-being. He is a representative of God's work. That work does not go on without God's servants doing it, and they cannot do it without support.

"But," says the missionary candidate, "I have no objection to being supported by God's people. My objection is to 'begging for support.' "

To this there are two answers. The candidate may join any one of many denominational mission boards in which little or no responsibility is placed upon him to raise support. This is appealing and doubtless has some valid advantages, but it is not without weaknesses. The second answer is to face up to some of the positive values found in having to raise your support. And in this regard, it is noteworthy that most of the largest and fastest-growing missionary organizations in the last fifty years have been "faith missions." Furthermore, it would be hard to refute the claim that the "personalized support" program has been one of the most important contributing factors in the growth of those missions.

There is little in the life of the Christian worker that will do more to promote a long-time interest in both giving and intercession on the part of the home church than personal relationship. And woe be to that soldier of the cross who enters the heat of battle without the intercession of many friends. Furthermore, any deep sense of God's leading should be accompanied by the confidence that when God guides, he also provides. "Raising one's support," is a challenge to faith and without faith it is difficult to please God.

Dr. Fenton shares this wise counsel with missionary candidates,

> "See yourself, under the present system, not as a huckster of your own services or as a promoter of your own support, but as one who has had firsthand contact with God and who has acted under a sense of divine compulsion—and who therefore has something to share with others, young and old. See your mission to the churches not as a money-raising junket but as a further fulfillment of the Great

> Commission; you are going
> because of a divine call—to share
> with others what you know
> of Jesus Christ."

When the missionary candidate looks on the
raising of his support as an opportunity to
prove his faith, to inform fellow Christians
of God's work, to inspire them to invest in
things of eternal consequence, and to
encourage them in their intercession for him
and the work of the Lord, then his deputation
is no longer a mountain but a ministry. In
addition, he will find himself making personal
friendships that will be of rich spiritual
benefit to him, to his friends, and to the
work he represents. There is no substitute
for friends who really care.

> "After all pious platitudes have
> been swept away," says Fenton,
> "you will need the friendship,
> the prayers, and the deep
> interest of God's people as you
> take up your missionary
> ministry. You will need these
> things more than you need your
> monthly support. And a period
> of deputation may be the means
> God will use to give you a wider
> circle of praying friends than
> you presently have."

There are today hundreds of missionaries
whose testimonies corroborate Bessie

Degerman's as she says,

> "I would not exchange for anything the faith-expanding experience I had of watching the Lord supply my needs for going to Japan. It has been one of the highlights of my missionary experience."

Are missionaries beggars? I guess the answer really depends upon our perspective of God's work and interpretation of his Word.

> And it is he who will supply all your needs from his riches in glory, because of what Christ Jesus has done for us.
> Philippians 4:19/*TLB*

MISSIONARY WORK OVERSEAS?!,...ARE YOU KIDDING?...I'M AFRAID OF SNAKES, ALLERGIC TO MOSQUITOES, I FLUNK LANGUAGES, I'M AFRAID TO FLY, GET SEASICK, DON'T MAKE FRIENDS, FAINT WHEN I GET SHOTS. MY HAIR GOES STRAIGHT IN DAMP WEATHER,...

Afraid of being
a missionary wife?
Then spend a few minutes
with this fresh outlook
on the subject.

 ## What!
Me a missionary
wife?

It has been facetiously said
that behind every successful
man is a surprised wife. In the
realm of missions it can be more
aptly said that behind most
successful missionary men are
godly wives. The missionary
wife is more than a glorified
baby sitter for her Adam. She is
a helpmate in all the glory
of that word.

Of all the birds, beasts, and
fish which God created, not one
was able to provide the answers
to Adam's physical, social,
academic, moral, and spiritual

needs. If Adam was to have a companion in the fullest meaning of that word, God would have to do something special. Adam's partner would have to be someone far more like Adam than any bird, beast, or fish.

For God, the operation was simple—a divine anaesthetic, the removal of a rib, and a creative word. Incidentally, if you are worried about the missing rib, relax! The floating ribs have the unique ability to regrow themselves.

When Eve stood in Adam's presence, he not only knew she was bone of his bone, but also that she was the only answer to making life meaningful to him. Together, Adam and Eve soon learned that their physical, social, academic, moral and religious well-being were inseparably related to their oneness. No other creature on earth could fulfill their physical and social desires, compete with their academic abilities, challenge their moral standards, or encourage them in their religious aspirations. These things could only be accomplished through fellowship with one another. Furthermore, of all God's creatures, they alone could have a communicative relationship with God.

Of course "the woman thou gavest me" has not always been a faithful companion. Like her mother Eve, she has sometimes fallen short of fulfilling her God-given responsibilities. However, more often than not she has proven to be a balance wheel, a place of refuge, a strong tower, an inspiration, and a source of spiritual strength to the man with whom she is mated. Before you reject the idea of being a missionary wife, you ought to consider the following.

A physical savior

A missionary wife will certainly be far more solicitous of her husband's physical well-being than the best paid servant could ever be. She works long hours to prepare his meals and make his house attractive and comfortable. She is concerned about how hard he works and how much sleep he gets. When he is sick she is more compassionate than a nurse. She is tender, thoughtful, and loving.

A moral savior

To put it bluntly, she satisfies his sexual appetites. Those appetites are real and when not satisfied, temptations to immorality are intensified. As an affectionate wife she helps to solve this moral problem through God-ordained expressions of love. Her intimate affection provides for him a deep satisfaction which rides victoriously over the strength of lust. "The heart of her husband doth safely trust in her" (Proverbs 31:11).

A social savior

Third, she is a social savior. The niceties

of human society most often reveal the feminine touch. Those societies in which women are down-trodden lack much of that which makes Christian society enjoyable. When the daughters of Eve become insensible to the good graces of Christian culture, all of society is degraded.

An emotional savior

Man's need for sharing his problems and privileges, joys and sorrows, is ageless and universal. In fact, this is exactly what the creation story is all about. Until Eve was created, Adam had no one with whom he could really identify, no one with whom to share himself. Fortunate is the missionary whose wife is always ready to mop up the spilled milk of disappointment and provide for him a listening ear into which he can pour his woes. With her, he divides his problems and multiplies his joys. She is his psychological haven.

An economic savior

Some wives are spendthrifts, but this is not characteristic of missionary women. They appreciate the blood, sweat, and tears their husbands have put into each dollar brought home. They protect the budget. They shop carefully. They look for bargains. They recognize that some of the dollars they spend came from sacrificial gifts. They know they are stewards of the provisions God sends their way. They tend to make sure that offerings for God and his work are not forgotten.

An academic savior

Sixth, she is an academic savior. She challenges her husband to good reading and continual study. She knows that if he is to be an alert missionary with a fruitful ministry, he must be a thorough student of the Word and of the world. He must be aware of the times and seasons in which he lives. She sacrificially foregoes times of fellowship with him for the sake of his academic advance.

A spiritual savior

This is surely the realm of her greatest contribution. Her personal love for and devotion to God are an inspiration to him. God is continually giving ear to her supplications in behalf of her husband. Her insistence on faithfulness to the missionary task is a gentle rebuke to him. The discipline of her private devotions and her steadfastness relative to the family altar encourage him. Her consistent efforts to raise her children in the nurture of the Word amazes him. Her spiritual example helps him to be his best for God.

It is little wonder then that the Scriptures instruct the Christian husband to love his wife as Christ loved the Church and gave himself for her. Obviously, there is no one else on earth so able to make his life meaningful. He does well to be mindful of her great contribution to him. He should often express his appreciation to her as his co-worker. He should not underestimate her gifts and abilities. He should not hesitate to place her in the limelight when occasion arises. He should encourage her in her efforts to improve herself. He should be faithful to her, provide for her, and love her "till death do us part."

Perhaps being a missionary wife carries with it greater privileges than you had realized. Besides the happy and holy responsibilities mentioned above, you will have the added joy of directly serving your Lord in children's meetings, women's classes, and in a dozen and one other ways. Looks like a rather "high calling," doesn't it?

> Be beautiful inside, in your hearts, with the lasting charm of a gentle and quiet spirit which is so precious to God. That kind of deep beauty was seen in the saintly women of old, who trusted God and fitted in with their husbands' plans.
> 1 Peter 3:4, 5/*TLB*

So you don't want
your children educated
in a missionary
boarding school?
It may not be
as bad as you think!

What!
Separated from
my children?

Someone has said that happiness
is being a missionary kid. But
not always! I know M.K.s* who
are frustrated, lonely, and
resentful. "I've been so lonely
in the States that I've turned to
dope," confessed a missionary
daughter. "Some of the M.K.s
on our campus have real
problems," said a college dean.
But these are far from typical
statements.

In contrast, Robert Porch,
headmaster of a missionary
academy in Peru, made a
survey of the alumni of his

*Missionary Kids

school. He wanted to know whether the graduates were maladjusted.

Here are the revealing results of his survey, published in the *Amazon Valley Indian*:

> 7 are active missionaries on the foreign field.
>
> 2 are attending theological seminary.
>
> 11 are attending Bible college— with several already committed to overseas service.
>
> 5 are working as trained nurses.
>
> 1 is still in nurses training.
>
> 1 is a pastor.
>
> 1 does administrative work in a prominent denomination.
>
> 5 of the girls have married ministerial students.
>
> 9 are attending university— several in preparation for the mission field.
>
> 2 are teaching elementary school.
>
> 3 are housewives.
>
> 2 are in the armed forces.
>
> 6 are in business.
>
> 1 says he is no longer interested in church.
>
> 9 did not respond—but we know of several who are in college and others who are married.

The record indicates a significant percentage of success. Neither

the credit nor the blame could be
laid to the mission school
entirely, but the point is made
about maladjustment. It seems
that M.K.s go where other
well-trained children go. And it
appears that they go just as
fast, just as far, and just as well.

In spite of a report like this there are scores
of Christian young couples who hold back
from the mission field because of convictions
against being separated from their children.
This is a grave problem, but it is sometimes
misunderstood. Though geographic separation
is often necessary, it is not always harmful.
Emotional separations that take place between
Christian parents and their children in the
States often are worse.

The wise missionary parent does not allow
distance to bring division. Faithful correspondence, telephone conversations where
possible, and frequent visits all help to main-
tain the parent-child relationship. The lines
of communication are kept open as parents
show vital interest in the details of their
child's experiences in school. Furthermore,
the child can feel he has a part in the work of
the parents if they keep him informed and
seek his prayers for their work. During vacation times they can involve him in various
ways in their work so that he feels he is
a missionary.

But let's hear from the M.K.s themselves. Their testimonies will help us to see the picture more clearly:

"I was born in the heart of Africa to missionary parents. In obedience to God's guidance they had entered the Zambezi Valley to tell those simple people of God's love.

"Not long after my second birthday, illness crept into our little group. Anxious weeks that followed included a long, hope-filled journey to the hospital. There my father died of typhoid fever. Yet, knowing that nothing sneaks by God, my mother returned to Rhodesia to carry on the work.

"Once again, I found myself in the midst of night noises, tropical storms, and dusky people. As I look back on those years, I remember the times that something inside whispered, 'Why, of all people, must I be an M.K.? And a fatherless one at that!' But these thoughts did not come often, being swallowed in the joy that tumbled in upon me. Mine was a life of high adventure.

"Before the age of twelve I had stood at the edge of that magnificent wonder, Victoria Falls. I played on the beaches in Mozambique, traveled through South Africa and Swaziland, the Madeira Islands, and England. Also mine to remember was the vast United States from coast to coast.

"Not only was mine a life of adventure. Early I learned the meaning of service. For many hours I watched missionary nurses minister to crowds of tired, miserable, sick people. I saw the love of Christ in their eyes and hands. At times it was my privilege to wrap a bandage or to hold a head while a tooth was pulled.

"Then it was time to further my education, and I returned to the United States to become a nurse. Now, preparation behind us, my husband and I have returned to serve Christ in South Africa.

"All this is mine because my parents were obedient to God's leading, regardless of the cost. I thank God for such a heritage."

A survey asked some M.K.s whether they felt they had been "robbed" by having to live overseas. Their answers are revealing:

A boy in the Orient said,

> "I feel I am better off than the
> average kid in America.
> It is a privilege."

A girl in the Philippines wrote,

> "If had my choice, I would put
> being a missionary's kid
> against anything else."

In a little different note tinged with delightful sarcasm, a missionary kid who spent her teen-age years in Taiwan admits,

> "Sure I have been robbed—
> robbed of spending all those
> hours sitting in front of a TV
> set, robbed of having 'Winston
> tastes good like a cigarette
> should' singing through my head
> constantly, robbed of American
> prejudice against dark skin
> and almond-shaped eyes,
> robbed of a school system
> designed to make everyone just
> like everyone else."

This is not to suggest that M.K.s don't have complaints. They do. And though separation from their parents is high on the list, the attitude toward them expressed by some

Christians in the States runs a close second. In this regard an M.K. shares some good advice:

> "First, treat us like normal kids. Do not expect us to be something we are not. Realize we have the same hang-ups, the same needs, the same desires as other kids; then do what you can to meet these needs or to help our parents to meet them.
>
> "Second, be genuine in your relationship with missionaries. Act toward them as you would toward other people. They are not superspiritual. Neither are they misfits who could not succeed in the United States. They are real people and we are resentful when our parents are not treated that way.
>
> "Third, pray for both the missionary and for his children. Because missionaries have responsibilities helping and counseling others, they have difficulty finding time and energy to minister to their own families. My father was constantly away from home. But I am firmly

> convinced that the prayers of my
> parents and those of other
> Christians helped meet needs
> created by his absence."

It can be wonderfully advantageous to be
raised on the foreign field, and many M.K.s
recognize this. They grow up bilingual as well
as bicultural.

One girl spoke for a number of the M.K.s
when she said,

> "Travel broadens one's outlook.
> You see things, meet people, im-
> portant and unimportant, and
> learn the way the other side of
> the world lives. It is like a fun
> education."

Speaking of school, one wrote,

> "Going to school with other
> races and with people of different
> religions has enriched my life
> and made me thankful I am a
> Christian. I would never have
> known how much Jesus did for
> me if I hadn't gone abroad.
> He is so neat and so few
> know it."

A boy wrote,

> "Being here on a foreign field I
> have seen the gospel in action
> and I realize it is not a white

52

> guy's religion. Also, being a
> missionary kid has helped my
> personality. I think I am more
> flexible and more adaptable and
> have less prejudice. I am not
> as limited in my philosophy
> and viewpoint about life. It also
> helped me to set right values."

It is often more difficult for parents to be separated from their children than vice versa. Some parents have been overprotective or have failed to impart to their children the excitement and joy of being workers together with God. This has led to problems. Other parents do have sincere questions as to the rightfulness of separation. But there is overwhelming evidence that happiness is often the inheritance of the missionary child. God has a way of doing extra things for the children of parents who have "left all to follow him."

So you don't want to be separated from your son (or daughter)? God was.

> "Anyone who wants to be my
> follower must love me far more
> than he does his own father,
> mother, wife, children, brothers,
> or sisters—yes, more than his
> own life—otherwise he cannot
> be my disciple."
> Luke 14:26/*TLB*

53

YOUNG LADY HOW ABOUT CONSIDERING A SHORT TERM MISSIONARY PROJECT OVERSEAS?
..WELL I MIGHT CONSIDER IT IF THEY HAVE MODERN FACILITIES, SWIMMING POOL, MOTEL ACCOMODATIONS, THAT SORT OF THING...

From a scriptural view
we are living in
an evangelized nation.
We are a people
with gospel surplus.

 What!
America
is evangelized?

Major premise:

God has commissioned the
church to bring the world
to Christ.

Minor premise:

There are still thousands in
America who have never been
brought to Christ.

Conclusion:

There is no reason for me to
consider overseas service.

Though the author of this syllogism may be sincere, he is obviously deluded. His major premise is false; therefore, his conclusion is in error. God has not commissioned the church to bring the world to Christ. This was not God's assignment to his people. It does not accurately describe the Great Commission.

God has commissioned the church to *take Christ to the world!* The church's responsibility is to make Christ available to all men. The intent of the Great Commission is to give to every man, woman, and child an intelligent opportunity to accept or reject Jesus Christ as personal Savior. This is a far cry from bringing the world to Christ.

Apparently the early believers were confused about this. It seems that they intended to stay in Jerusalem until all Jerusalem was won to Christ. Knowing this would never happen, the Lord allowed persecution to scatter the believers and drive them out of the city. It is noteworthy that each forward step in the ongoing of the gospel, as seen in Acts, was a traumatic experience for the church. Judea was not evangelized until the believers were forcibly driven into the area. Samaria received no gospel witness until a special act of divine guidance took Philip into that region.

Though the Lord's commission to his followers was outlined in easily-understood words (Jerusalem—Judea—Samaria and the uttermost part of the earth), the Jewish converts to Christianity found it quite impossible to believe that the Lord really meant the gospel for the Gentiles. Even Peter would never have gone to a Gentile apart from a special act of divine compulsion. His vision from heaven and trip to Caesarea culminated in the conversion of Cornelius and his household. And then, after returning to Jerusalem, he found it necessary to describe his experiences in detail in order to convince the leaders of the "mother" church that God was bringing Gentiles to himself.

Back of some of this confusion lay the false concept that God had commissioned the church to bring the world to Christ. And as far as the Jewish converts were concerned, the only world was the Jewish world. It was, of course, obvious to them that there were still many in Jerusalem and Judea who were unsaved, even though the news of the crucifixion and the resurrection of Christ had been gossiped throughout the whole land. Though 3,000 had come to Christ at Pentecost and 5,000 shortly after, there were many unsaved still in Jerusalem, Nazareth, Bethlehem, and every other Judean city. So why go farther? If Christ had commissioned the church to bring the world to Christ, it was normal for the believers not to move beyond the borders of their own area with their witness.

The fact is, all the world will never be brought to Christ. But it can be said dogmatically that Christ must be taken to all the world. Even a cursory study of Acts and of church history shows that this is what God has commissioned his followers to do. The Good News is to be shared with all nations in order that all men in all languages may have an intelligent opportunity to accept or reject the Savior.

In the 19th chapter of Acts we are introduced to Paul's ministry in the city of Ephesus. Verse ten reads,

> "And this continued by the space of two years so that all they which dwelt in Asia heard the word of the Lord Jesus, both Jews and Greeks."

The Asia of Paul's day was a province located in the western end of what is now Turkey. It was a well-populated area containing such cities as Philadelphia, Laodicea, Thyatira, Troas, and Ephesus. Paul did not claim that all those who dwelt in Asia were won to Christ. He left thousands of unsaved behind him. He simply claimed that as a result of what God had wrought in Ephesus, the word of the Lord Jesus was made available to all the Jews and Greeks in the province of Asia.

In Romans 15 we have a more striking illustration of this same principle. In reporting what the Lord had done among the Gentiles through him, Paul says,

> "So that from Jerusalem and
> round about unto Illyricum, I
> have fully preached the
> gospel of Christ."

Illyricum is present-day Yugoslavia. The road
distance between Yugoslavia and Jerusalem
is approximately 2,000 miles.

Paul does not for one moment suggest that
everyone within that vast area was brought
to Christ. He left many an unconverted
person behind him as he traveled to Illyricum.
He had, however, been used of the Lord
to plant churches in Galatia, Cappadocia,
Asia, Greece, and Illyricum. Corinth,
Thessalonica, Philippi, Crete, Iconium, Lystra,
and Antioch were some of the lighthouses
of the gospel that had been erected for the
glory of God. The apostle knew that if there
were people in that stretch of territory reaching from Jerusalem to Illyricum who had a
desire to become acquainted with Jesus
Christ, they could do so through the groups
of believers he had left behind.

The little epistle of 1 Thessalonians gives
another illustration of the fact that God has
not commissioned the church to bring the
world to Christ but has commissioned the
church to take Christ to the world.

Paul's stay in Thessalonica had been brief.
His preaching, however, had been accompanied

by the power of the Holy Spirit. As a result, a goodly number had turned to God from idols. They had received the word of the Lord "in much affliction with joy of the Holy Ghost" and had then become examples "to all that believe in Macedonia and Achaia." Furthermore, their testimony was so spread abroad that Paul felt it was no longer necessary for him to return to that area. It is not that there were no unsaved left in Greece. Paul knew there were many. He was confident, however, that the gospel was available to them.

There is probably no country in all of history that has enjoyed so much gospel surplus as the United States of America. It cannot be denied that the gospel is available to all men in this country. No man is farther away than a radio switch from the gospel message— no farther than a short drive to a church that is faithful in preaching the Good News. This is not to suggest that there are not thousands of men and women in the States who do not understand the gospel. There are Ph.D.s on our university campuses who have little or no comprehension of the meaning of the crucifixion and resurrection of Jesus Christ. But their ignorance does not stem from a lack of available information. If they do not understand the gospel, if they are blind to it, their blindness grows out of neglect or willful ignorance.

Perhaps a few statistics will help put the

picture in proper perspective. There are 70 million Protestants in the U.S.A., and that is more than twice as many as in any other country in the world. And think of these facts:

> There are more people in Sunday school on any given Sunday in America than in all the rest of the world.

> There are more young people in our Bible institutes and Bible colleges than in all the rest of the world. Though the population of Russia is greater than that of the United States, there is only one evangelical Russian-language Bible institute in the world. The sixty students in that school stand in bold contrast to the 60,000 students in similar schools in this country.

> We have more seminarians than all the other countries of the world put together. There are more students in just one of our seminaries than in all the seminaries of Europe and Asia combined. In just one of our Bible institutes, there are more students than in all such schools on the continent of Africa.

> We have many times more hours

of gospel broadcasting than
any other nation.

There is more evangelical
literature printed in English
than in all the other languages
of the world combined.

We have more Baptist
congregations in the
United States than we have
Protestant missionaries overseas.

Though Americans make up only 1/17th of
the world's population, they enjoy a gospel
surplus unsurpassed by any nation during
all the centuries of church history. We own
268 million radio sets, and 6,700 radio
stations. Almost without exception, those
stations carry anywhere from one to a dozen
gospel broadcasts a week. We have 5,000
church-related camps, and 3,000 church-
related schools.

Add to this the work of our Bible societies,
Christian publishers, and free literature
distribution programs. Then think of the
various nationwide ministries to children, high
school, and college young people. It cannot
be denied that the message of God's love
in Christ is available to all men in America.
From a biblical view, we are living in an
evangelized nation—evangelized as no other
nation has ever been.

To suggest that the United States is just as

much a mission field as any other country is to promote a half-truth. If by that statement one means that an unsaved American is as unsaved as an unsaved Chinese, the statement is true. But if the statement implies that the remedy is as available to the Chinese as to the American, nothing could be farther from the truth. There are millions of people in the world to whom the message of God's saving grace is just not available in any form, and that is not true in the United States.

This does not mean that we as American believers can fold our hands and forget all about witnessing to our neighbors. Wherever God has placed us we are to be the light of the world—we are to be his witnesses. Recognizing this fact, however, it must be our determined purpose to get the gospel out to the millions who do not now have an opportunity to hear it. To proclaim the Good News to men and women in lands where it is not now available must be our priority, for to whom much has been given much shall be required.

> But all the while my ambition has been to go still farther, preaching where the name of Christ has never yet been heard, rather than where a church has already been started by someone else.
> Romans 15:20/*TLB*

What did the early
church do about the
economic problems of
the Roman Empire?
What did she do
about injustice and
social inequalities?
Was she right?

What!
Other ghettos?

So you're interested in our
American ghettos? And why
shouldn't you be? How can we
as Christians stand idly by
while thousands of our fellow
citizens live under the difficult
conditions in which they find
themselves in the inner city?
How can we send missionaries
to Latin America and neglect
the Latins in our own country?
Is it possible that our apparent
concern for reaching the blacks
in the Congo is real if we are
indifferent toward the blacks in
the United States? These

questions deserve studied attention by all who profess to love Christ. We must not be indifferent to anyone in need. But that "in need" business may be the rub.

What kind of needs are we talking about? Is the church's first concern to be the economic, educational, or political need of people? Or has the church of Jesus Christ been called upon to respond to a need that is more basic than other needs? In other words, are economic, academic, social, and political needs symptoms or are they the real thing? Are they the root of our problems or are they the fruit of a deeper problem?

It is preposterous to suggest that the church was ever commissioned to take care of the economic needs of the world. Though the church has repeatedly and generously responded to famine and other crisis situations, it is apparent that it is in no position to solve the economic problems of even a large city, much less those of a nation or of the world. Having acknowledged this, it must be said that history bears irrefutable proof that the spread of the gospel has always been accompanied by a generous and sacrificial compassion for the poor. Witness the billions of dollars given by the American public to economic aid programs around the world. Though politics is also involved, much of that which has been given has been given on the plain level of Christian compassion. The same quality of compassion is not found among people uninfluenced by Christianity.

The Scriptures are consistent in their teaching that sin is the root of man's problems and that the problems themselves are the fruit. They are the symptoms of that which is basically wrong. It is for this reason that morality, justice, and economic equality cannot be legislated. And who can deny that when the church faces up to the sin problem, it is following in the footsteps of the Master.

At the birth of Jesus it was said,

> "Thou shalt call his name Jesus
> for he shall save his people
> from their sins."

John the Baptist later introduced Jesus Christ to the world as

> "the Lamb of God who takes
> away the sin of the world."

Jesus stated his purpose for being on earth when he said,

> "For the Son of Man is come to
> seek and to save that which
> was lost."

It is noteworthy that nothing is said in these statements of purpose that directly relates to the social, economic, or academic conditions of people. Jesus did not promise to take away the illiteracy or poverty of the world. His primary goal was not to educate the ignorant or to bring about economic equality. He knew the root problem was sin and that these other issues could not and would not be taken care of until the root problem was dealt with. This clarifies our understanding of the church's basic responsibility to our ghettos—mainly, to share the gospel in all of its liberating power with the people therein. This must be the first step. Injustice and immorality, discrimination, social and economic inequalities will never disappear as long as men's hearts are selfish and egocentric.

And, while thinking of ghettos, we will do well to remember that our world is now a global village. This makes it easy for us to look at other ghettos. For example, the little country of Haiti has a population exceeding five million people, 95% of whom are of African descent. They are crowded together in a ratio of 428 persons per square mile, and 90% of them are illiterate. The per capita gross income is approximately $70 a year. Doesn't it sound like one large ghetto?

Bangladesh is about the size of Florida, yet it has a population of over 75 million people. This means the entire population of New York, Texas, California, Oregon, and Washington could all be placed in the State of Florida and still not surpass that of Bangladesh.

Per capita income in Bangladesh is about $50 a year. A large percentage of the population is living on a level of five cents per day per person. Eighty percent of the people are illiterate. Bangladesh is one huge, hungry, semiliterate ghetto.

There are over 200 million people living in ghetto conditions in India. Some 70% of the families of Calcutta's six million people live in one room. Furthermore, India's "caste discrimination makes American race relations appear benevolent." According to one observer, India's cities are "cluttered to the point of paralysis by the daily increment of babies from heaven and immigrants from villages."

Every cement jungle in the world today has its skid row, its slum, and its ghetto. There are very few ghetto families in other countries who would not jump at the chance of trading places with American ghetto families. The question is, is it the church's mandate to attack the economic, academic, and social problems found therein? Does the church have the manpower and money to tackle the job? Or does the fulfilling of the Great Commission relate to something more basic to human need?

The Book of Acts gives us the history of the early church in action. It is the story of first-generation believers obeying the command of the Savior as they saw and understood it. Interestingly enough, there is no instance in Acts in which the early church directly attacked the academic and economic problems of their day. It cannot be doubted that large cities such as Antioch, Ephesus, Corinth, Athens, and Rome had their share of slums and ghettos. They had their slaves, their unemployed, poverty-stricken, and semiliterates. Apparently the early church's response to these needs was to proclaim the gospel. They did this in full confidence that when men and women become new creatures in Christ, their surroundings will be affected for the better. Furthermore, they did it in the full assurance that they were obeying the commission God had given them.

All of this is another way of saying that it is right for the Christian to be concerned about the ghettos of the United States as well as others around the world. We must, however, rightly discern the source of that concern. Does it grow out of an interest in the physical and economic welfare of people? Or is it a spiritual concern which relates to their eternal welfare? Can we make our greatest contribution to the world in which we live by providing bread, or by providing *The Bread?* Can it be denied that God's instruction to his people gives priority to the latter?

> One night the Lord spoke to
> Paul in a vision and told him,
> "Don't be afraid! Speak out!
> Don't quit! For I am with you
> and no one can harm you.
> Many people here in this
> city belong to me."
> Acts 18:9, 10/TLB

Is it possible that Christianity is the only true religion? What about Islam, Buddhism and the other great religions?

What! Other religions?

Four hundred and fifty million Moslems and four hundred million Hindus can't be wrong—or can they? Hinduism was practiced by thousands of people centuries before Christ was born and Islam came into being twelve centuries ago. How could such ancient and revered religions be anything but right? And what about Confucianism, Buddhism, Shintoism, Taoism, and Animism with their millions of adherents? Surely it is not possible that these great religions are false.

Well, let's remember first that the antiquity of an ideology is no proof of its truthfulness. Falsehood is as old as truth and sin is as old as mankind. The existence of the "Father of Lies" predates man's history. The lie has always been with us and there is no lie bigger than the religious lie.

In the second place, it doesn't take an academic genius to realize that not all of the world's religions—ancient and contemporary—can be true. In many cases, they plainly contradict each other and two contradictory statements cannot both be true. Truth does not contradict itself. If, for example, you insist that five plus six is eleven and I insist that it is thirteen or any other figure other than eleven, one of us is wrong. In this case (as usual), you are right.

Looking at this mathematical equation carefully, you will discover that it presents four possibilities.

1

You and I could both be wrong.

2

You could be right and I wrong.

3

I could be right and you wrong.

Both of us could be right. In this latter case, we would both have to come up with the answer—eleven.

Now let's see how these principles apply to religious ideologies. Let's compare Hinduism with Islam. India's 400 million Hindus worship myriads of gods. Idolatry is an integral part of their religious philosophy and practice. Islam, on the other hand, is a monotheistic (one god) religion. Islam's millions (Moslems) would rather die than bow the knee to an idol. In other words, Islam says idolatry is a sure way to hell while Hinduism says it is a sure way to heaven. Obviously, both of these ideologies cannot be true in any ultimate sense of the word. They could, however, both be false. Or one could be true and the other false.

Perhaps a look at the more salient teachings of these great religions will help us come up with some right conclusions.

Hinduism

Hinduism is a pantheistic philosophy which teaches that God is all, and all is God. It eventuates, however, in a polytheistic practice in which any and everything can be worshiped. You have heard of India's holy cow. The Hindu scriptures teach that "all who kill cows shall rot in hell for as many years as there are hairs on the slain cow." But the cow is not the only "holy" thing in India. The sun, the stars, and the moon, the rivers and the lakes, the birds, beasts, and creeping things, even the trees, the sticks, and stones can be objects of worship. Like the Athenians of old, India seems to be given "wholly to idolatry" (Acts 17).

Hinduism teaches transmigration of soul and, hence, all of life is sacred. Whether, therefore, it is a grain-eating peacock, a bubonic plague-carrying rat, a deadly poisonous cobra, a garden-destroying monkey, or an unproductive cow, it must not be killed. Just imagine the terrible contribution toward poverty this philosophy of life makes. The rat population in India is several times that of the people and they say that six rats will eat as much grain as one person.

Hinduism teaches that certain groups of people came from the head of God, others from the shoulders and chest of God, others from his hips and loins while yet others came from the feet of God. Then there are the outcastes who came from beneath God's feet. India's caste system has grown out of the soil of this concept.

Basic to Hinduism is the belief that men go through innumerable cycles of reincarnation, passing from "vegetables to animals, from animals to humans, from one human body to another, sometimes up the scale and sometimes down until they are pure enough to return to Brahma, the spiritual source." Bathing in sacred rivers, burning incense at various shrines, saying prayers and doing good works affect each succeeding incarnation.

Hinduism has a trinity in which the four-headed Brahma abides as the creator and, "presides from the mythical Mt. Meru where he lives with his peacock-riding wife, Sarasvati." Vishnu, the preserver, also lives on Mt. Meru with his wife, Lakshmi. He "rides through the heavens on a garuda (a man-bird), but periodically, he has incarnated himself on the earth as a fish, or a porpoise." Shiva, the destroyer, lives on Mt. Kailas. His wife may appear as Parvati, a graceful woman, or as Durga, a fierce lion-riding woman, or as Kali, a blood-thirsty goddess who demands blood sacrifices. So much for Hinduism.

Islam

Now let's look at Islam. This great religion with its more than 450 million followers was founded by Mohammed in the early part of the seventh century. It is not certain that Mohammed could either read or write, but he did rebel against the idolatry into which he was born.

The sacred book of Islam is the Koran. It is basically a compilation of the things

Mohammed said. The "Five Pillars of Islam" as given in the Koran are:

> 1. Confession that there is no god but Allah, and Mohammed is his prophet
> 2. Ritual prayers observed five times daily, facing Mecca
> 3. Almsgiving—2½ percent of the gross wealth
> 4. Fasting during the daylight hours of the month of Ramadan
> 5. Making one pilgrimage to Mecca during the lifetime, if possible

To the Moslem, heaven is a place filled with gardens, fountains, flowing wines, and lovely virgins. Hell is a place of fire, pestilential winds, and scalding water. When a Moslem dies, the following brief catechism is whispered into his deaf ears: "Who is thy God? Allah. What is thy religion? Islam. Who is its prophet? Mohammed."

There is probably no other religion so heavily weighted with fatalism. To the Moslem, "What has happened has happened and what will happen will happen." God in sovereign caprice has chosen or rejected whomsoever he will. The Moslem's basic hope is that somehow his good deeds may outweigh his evil. It will then be his good fate to get to heaven, if God has so elected.

History (both ancient and contemporary) seems to demonstrate that Islam has contributed little to the academic, material, moral, and social advance of its adherents. It is not unrealistic to say that economic poverty, academic darkness, disrespect for womanhood, and moral laxity have characterized Islamic nations. Those Moslem countries that are today veering away from the Koran are becoming enlightened and progressive.

Now, take a second look at Hinduism and Islam. Note how greatly their doctrines vary. Obviously, they can't both be true. And where and how (if at all) do they compare with the Christian message? But before answering that question, perhaps we ought to glance at several of the other great religions.

Buddhism

Buddhism was founded by Siddhartha Gautama a little more than 500 years before Christ. The goal of the true Buddhist is to eliminate all desire. This is done by sublimation and sacrifice and leads to a final impersonal ultimate reality. But, "the road is hard, and one is bound for many lives to the cosmic merry-go-round, which is called the Wheel of Rebirth."

Though there are millions of Buddhists in India, China, and Japan, Buddhism has its strongest hold in Ceylon, Thailand, and

Tibet. These countries are filled with monasteries in which rosary-counting monks practice celibacy, poverty, and renunciation. The Buddhist layman may receive merit through offerings, pilgrimages, meditation, by feeding the monks and helping in the upkeep of the shrines.

Salvation to the Buddhist has nothing to do with deliverance from the penalty or power of sin. There is no concept of forgiveness, redemption, atonement, justification, or glorification in this religion. The idolatry of the religion is seen mainly in the worship of images of the Buddha.

You might do well to think twice relative to the choice of being raised in a Thailand monastery over against that of growing up on the doorsteps of a Christian church.

Confucianism

Confucius was a great teacher and editor of the classical writings of China. He died in the year 479 B.C., saying to those about him, "The great mountain must fall. The strong timber is broken. The wise man fades as does the plant."

Confucius did not think of himself as the founder of a new religion; but early in our present century (1906) the "last Manchu emperor elevated him to position beside Heaven and Earth, the highest objects of worship."

Confucianism is really a system of human ethics involving filial piety. It is an attempt to work out an "ideal standard of conduct" in all human interaction both with the living and the dead. The worship of the spirits of departed loved ones is therefore much a part of this religion. There is little or no thought of an eternal God having any kind of a personal relationship with either sinner or saint in Confucianism.

Taoism

Salvation to the follower of Confucius lies "in the resigning of one's will to Tao— 'the Way of Nature.' " Taoism, practiced so vigorously in Japan, is basically ancestor worship. It is possible to be a good follower of Confucius and a good Taoist at the same time.

So there you have it—a touch of four of the world's great religions. And if you have read carefully, you have noted their common denominator. They are all human attempts to obtain heavenly goals. And in some cases even the heavenly goals seem to be omitted.

Christianity

Salvation by works is characteristic of all religions except Christianity; everything depends on human effort. And this stands in bold contrast to the message of Jesus

Christ. His message pinpoints man's depravity
and impotency and leaves man helpless and
hopeless with insurmountable odds against
him. It teaches man that he cannot forgive
his own sin or wash the wickedness from
his heart. At the same time the message of
Christ teaches man that God in unfathomable
love has made perfect provision for man's
perfect salvation.

Christianity, therefore, is not one of the
comparative religions. It stands in bold
contrast to all other religion. It either is
what it claims to be—*the only way*—or it
is an enormous fraud. As a Christian you
have already cast your vote. Now go out
and raise your flag.

> There is salvation in no one
> else! Under all heaven there
> is no other name for men to
> call upon to save them.
> Acts 4:12/*TLB*

If there is no other
name than Jesus whereby
men may enter heaven,
then give the idea of
becoming a missionary
your deepest thoughts
and most earnest prayers.

 What!
Neo-universalism?

Heaven? Yes!
Hell? No!
"I can't really believe the
heathen will go to hell. In fact,
I am not sure there is a hell.
I have a genuine hang-up on this
condemnation bit. I don't
believe any man is bad enough
to deserve all the Bible teaches
hell is. Purgatory, perhaps,
but hell, no."

This statement expresses the
conviction of many Christians,
and some of those who make it
believe all who are not believers
in Christ will ultimately be

annihilated. Others feel that all men will at last be saved. This is the doctrine of universalism.

Neo-universalism teaches that because Jesus Christ died for the whole world, he will ultimately bring all men to himself. In reality, it claims that all men are already saved because of the shed blood of Christ. The purpose of missions, then, is simply to inform men that they are saved. Such a theological position is not without apparent scriptural grounds. For example, there is this passage from the Gospels:

> "And I, if I be lifted up from the earth, will draw all men unto me" (John 12:32).

The neo-universalist concludes from this that because Christ was lifted up (at Calvary), he will draw all men unto himself.

In the book of Acts, the universalist turns to the third chapter and borrows the following from Peter's sermon:

> "Whom the heaven must receive until the times of restitution of all things . . ." (Acts 3:21).

From the Epistles he takes such phrases as,

> "For as in Adam all die, even so in Christ shall all be made alive" (1 Corinthians 15:22).

> "To wit, that God was in
> Christ, reconciling the world
> unto himself" (2 Corinthians
> 5:19).

> "And, having made peace
> through the blood of his cross,
> by him to reconcile all things
> unto himself . . ."
> (Colossians 1:20).

> ". . . not willing that any should
> perish . . ." (2 Peter 3:9).

Separated from their respective contexts, these
verses appear to claim that ultimately all
men will be saved. But the Bible is its own
best commentary. Scripture must explain
Scripture. The verse in 2 Peter, just referred
to, illustrates this. The proponents of
neo-universalism say that because God is
not willing that any should perish, no one
will therefore perish. The complete verse,
however, says that it is God's desire that

> "all should come to
> repentance."

Why repentance? Is repentance necessary
to men who are already saved? The whole
context of the verse is against a universalistic
theology.

It cannot by any stretch of the imagination
be denied that Jesus Christ taught eternal
punishment as well as eternal life. In fact,

he had as much to say about condemnation
as about salvation. He who is divine love
incarnate had as much to say about hell
as about heaven. He undeniably believed
that hell was a reality and that men were
going there. He also believed that his
finished work at Calvary could save men from
eternal condemnation, but this salvation was
to be a reality only to those who turned
in repentance toward God and placed their
faith in him.

There are large portions of Scripture which
become completely meaningless if universalism
is true. Jesus' account of the rich man and
Lazarus (Luke 16) is one of those. In it,
the Lord categorically states that between
the rich man and Lazarus

> "there is a great gulf fixed:
> so that they which would pass
> from hence to you cannot;
> neither can they pass to us, that
> would come from thence."

The rich man then pleads with Abraham to
send Lazarus to his five brothers,

> "that he may testify unto them,
> lest they also come into this
> place of torment."

Obviously the sending of Lazarus to the
five brothers on earth would be meaningless
if they were already destined to heaven
apart from any message Lazarus could give
to them.

This same principle is suggested by Christ's statement to the dying thief,

> "Today shalt thou be with me
> in paradise."

It is clear from that episode that one thief was to spend eternity with Christ and the other was to be separated therefrom. Back of the eternal fellowship with Christ which was to be enjoyed by the first thief was a repentant cry of faith. If before his statement of faith he was on his way to heaven anyway, his conversation with Christ was obsolete before it took place (Luke 23:39-43).

The teaching of neo-universalism implies that Jesus made a mistake when he said to Nicodemus,

> "You must be born again"

for

> "that which is born of the flesh
> is flesh; and that which is
> born of the Spirit is spirit."

The fact is,

> "flesh and blood cannot
> inherit the kingdom of heaven."

Furthermore, it is impossible to understand the teachings of such verses as John 3:15,

> "That whosoever believeth in him
> should not perish, but have
> eternal life."

And John 3:18,

> "He that believeth not is
> condemned already, because he
> hath not believed in the name
> of the only begotten Son of God."

How does one interpret the following verses
in light of neo-universalistic claims?

> "Enter ye in at the strait gate:
> for wide is the gate, and broad
> is the way, that leadeth to
> destruction, and many there be
> which go in thereat: because
> strait is the gate, and narrow is
> the way, which leadeth unto
> life, and few there be that
> find it" (Matthew 7:13, 14).

Or these verses:

> "And I saw the dead, small and
> great, stand before God; and
> the books were opened: and
> another book was opened, which
> is the book of life: and the
> dead were judged out of those
> things which were written in the
> books, according to their works.
> And the sea gave up the dead
> which were in it; and death and
> hell delivered up the dead which
> were in them: and they were
> judged every man according
> to their works. And death and

> hell were cast into the lake of
> fire. This is the second death.
> And whosoever was not found
> written in the book of life was
> cast into the lake of fire"
> (Revelation 20:12-15).

If neo-universalism is true, then all men are
really just robots. If the Hindu and the
Moslem, the Buddhist and the atheist are
all going to heaven, whether or not they
have chosen to go, then what room is left
for the free will of man?

If Judas (the son of perdition) is going to
spend eternity with Paul, (the flaming
evangelist), then Paul made a big mistake
in preaching the gospel so long and so hard
and at such great cost. He firmly believed
that men who did not hear could not believe
and that those who did not believe could
not be saved (Romans 10:13-15). He labored
under a holy "woe is me if I preach not the
gospel" compulsion. He was constrained by
the Spirit of God to make the love of God
available to all men.

Until the time of his conversion Paul believed
he had done his pious best to win eternity
for himself. But his conversion taught him
that men must become new creatures in
Christ Jesus. In the light of this, he paid every
conceivable price including the "supreme
sacrifice" to give men and women an intelligent opportunity to accept Christ as their

personal Savior. He did not do this just so they as Jews, Greeks, or barbarians might be able to better enjoy time. He did it because he knew their eternal destiny depended upon it.

Paul firmly believed in the consistent teaching of Scripture concerning the total depravity of human nature. His Holy Spirit-given teaching, found in the first three chapters of Romans, leaves us with no question concerning the fact that all have sinned and come short of God's righteous demands. He knew that if man was ever to enjoy eternal life, it would have to come as a gift from God. He accepted his Lord's definition of eternal life,

> "And this is life eternal, that
> they might know thee the only
> true God, and Jesus Christ,
> whom thou hast sent"
> (John 17:3).

Every student of Scripture knows that:

1

Men are lost, not because they haven't heard of Christ or haven't received him, but because they are sinners.

2

Men suppress the knowledge of God which they have through nature and through conscience. They do not live up to the light they have.

3

God is not obliged to save anyone. All men deserve hell. God's judgments are always righteous.

4

If any man of any generation in any country is ever to be saved, it is the grace of God alone that makes his salvation possible.

If you are a neo-universalist and believe that ultimately all men of all religious philosophies will go to heaven, then forget missions. If, on the other hand, you accept the Scriptures and believe that there is no other name given under heaven whereby men must be saved than the name of Jesus (Acts 4:12), then give the idea of becoming a missionary your best thoughts and deepest prayers.

> And this is the way to have eternal life—by knowing you, the only true God, and Jesus Christ, the one you sent to earth!
> John 17:3/*TLB*

I'D LIKE TO TALK TO YOU ABOUT SERVICE OVERSEAS...
NOW WAIT A MINUTE!,... I DIDN'T BURN MY DRAFT CARD!..

Whether it is the sword
of the preacher's tongue,
the author's pen,
or the layman's money,
it is to be used in a
more significant cause
than lopping off the ear
of Malchus or the
head of a Communist.

What!
Witness to
communists?

Not since the days of the
Crusades in Europe has there
been such a ferment among
Christians to preserve the
kingdom of God on earth.
In those days the cry was to
save the Holy Land from
desecration by the followers of
Islam. Today the cry is to save
the world from communism.
As a result religious
anti-communism crusades are
growing larger and louder by
the minute. It has become

increasingly popular in Christian circles to join a "holy crusade" against the Red scourge. The new "knights-in-bright-armor" have discovered that it is a popular and highly profitable venture to mount the white horse of capitalism, to sound an alarm of holy war, and to ride off in pursuit of the enemy.

Consequently, many pastors today receive a steady monotonous flow of literature purporting to give them the "last word" on communism. On the one hand, they are warned that communism is about to take over the American pulpit. On the other hand, it is the American university student who is the prime target of this atheistic philosophy. On the one hand, they are assured that our press is controlled by leftists and, on the other, that our federal government is infiltrated by Communist spies. On the one hand, communism is America's No. 1 enemy while, on the other, it is the Antichrist.

While much of this is devastatingly accurate and while Christians need to raise their voices and exercise the power of their vote against communism, yet those things which would tend to dissipate their ability to positively proclaim the gospel must be guarded against. Any church-sponsored anti-communism crusade which alienates the Christian from reaching the Communist for Christ must be watched with care.

Having said these things, I make haste to add that I hold no brief for communism. The writings of Lenin, Marx, Engels and the other proponents of Communist theories are totally untenable. Their materialistic and atheistic concepts stand in bold contrast to the teachings of the Holy Scriptures. As a Christian, I am antagonistic toward any teaching that shakes its fist in the face of God and denies the essential dignity of human personality.

But who can deny that anti-communism crusades are today dissipating the time, strength, and money of thousands of Christians? In the lives of some, anti-communism conversation has usurped Bible study. Anti-communism movements have supplanted missions. A warm and zealous witness, which at one time gave world evangelism its priority, has in some hearts been dethroned by a neurotic negativism which spends its energy fighting communism. An anti-communism meeting will draw 1,000 people while a Bible study or prayer meeting draws ten.

If the issue of communism is basically and truly political, then it is the government's responsibility to keep her people informed of its dangers. Though our government may be delinquent in this matter, who can deny that every medium of mass information is being used to acquaint us with the dangers of "Public Enemy No. 1." Where is the American citizen who is not aware of what Uncle Sam is doing both on a domestic and on an international basis, to expose communism? Where is the citizen who is not aware that $70 billion of our tax money is spent on military maintenance and buildup? Where is the daily paper that doesn't headline every move of the enemy?

The Old Testament prophets did not organize anti-Persian, nor anti-Babylonian movements. Though the political and religious aspects of those great empires were distasteful to them, the prophets spent their time endeavoring to correct the spiritual condition of Israel. Furthermore, where is the prophet who did not recognize that those godless empires were instruments in the hands of a sovereign God for the accomplishment of his own purposes in the world?

Unfortunately, religious anti-communism crusades have a way of equating Christianity with capitalism. They equate democracy with Christ and communism with the Antichrist. Such equations are devastating to the work of world evangelism in some countries.

Take, for example, Argentina. Her twenty million people pride themselves in their ability to think for themselves. They recognize the evils of both capitalism and communism. They sincerely question the advisability of becoming either pro-Western or pro-

Communist. Within their borders they have to live with two aggressive pressure groups—the Communist Party and the Roman Catholic Church.

In many Latin American minds the Roman Church, Christianity, democracy, and capitalism are synonymous. They have not experienced the live-and-let-live brand of democracy enjoyed in Protestant nations. The only capitalism they know has been despotic and tyrannical. It has often fostered class distinction and stifled freedom of thought, press, and religion. This type of "capitalism" has been pointedly illustrated in our western ally, Spain, where the basic freedoms have been denied to those who are not Catholic. In some Catholic countries 90 percent of the wealth is owned by 10 percent of the population.

Because of the political, economic, and educational programs of the Roman Church, there are thousands today in Latin America who are ready to align themselves with communism. A missionary friend suggests that many Latins "honestly feel they would have to sacrifice less character and would have less to lose under communism." This explains in part why Communist parties thrive in Roman Catholic countries.

It is a simple matter for the Christian in the United States to take sides against communism or Romanism. What would that same Christian do if he lived in a land where his alignment with either alternative was simply a choice between two evils, where he and his church would face the possibility of liquidation regardless of which group was in power?

There are those who say, "But isn't communism atheistic?" Of course it is, and for this reason we hate it. But who is there to argue that atheism is any more anti-Christ than polytheism, pantheism, or some forms of monotheism? Who is there to say that the teachings of communism are any more repulsive to God than those of Hinduism, Islam, Romanism, or theological liberalism?

Nor have anti-communism crusades been devoid of an anti-Communist spirit, which in turn reflects an anti-Russian or an anti-Chinese attitude. God's people need to beware of hating the Christless, regardless of their race, economic philosophy, or religion.

Christ's kingdom is not of this world, and we are of his kingdom. Our responsibility is to proclaim the gospel and to bring men and women into that kingdom over which he is King of kings and Lord of lords. We are to share the good news of God's grace to all men, including Communists.

We dare not be sidetracked.

> "I urge you . . . to preach the
> Word of God,"

Paul wrote to Timothy.

> "Never lose your sense of
> urgency, in season or out of
> season. Prove, correct and
> encourage, using the utmost
> patience in your teaching—
> go on steadily preaching the
> gospel and carry out to the full
> the commission that God
> gave you" (2 Timothy 4:2-5,
> Phillips).

In 1 Timothy 2:1-4 we are told that supplications, prayers, intercessions, and giving
of thanks should be made for all men,
for kings, and for all who are in authority.
The motivation for this is two-fold:

> 1. That we may lead quiet and
> peaceable lives, and
> 2. that men may be saved and
> come to the knowledge
> of the truth.

It is only reasonable to concede that those
prayers and supplications should include
those who are against us as well as those
who are with us. Perhaps Communist rulers
need to be included in our praying along
with capitalist rulers.

The apostles did not consume their energy
in combating the heinous powers of the

Roman Empire. The early church did not dissipate its time or money in anti-Nero crusades. The Lord Jesus Christ warned his followers about wolves in sheep's clothing but did not lead them into an anti-Roman Empire movement. He plainly taught them that his kingdom was not of this world. He clearly and repeatedly showed them that theirs was the positive imperative of proclaiming the gospel of a new citizenship.

When the Son of God was brought to trial in the world's judgment, he was asked,

> "Art thou the King of the Jews?"

His answer was,

> "My kingdom is not of this world: if my kingdom were of this world, then would my servants fight . . ."
> (John 18:36).

If our Lord's kingdom were of this world, then certainly it would be our responsibility to fight for its expansion and preservation. But his kingdom is not of this world, hence the public lifting of the sword by the servant of the Lord in anti-religio-political crusades does little more than cut off the ear of the high priest's servant. Whether it is the sword of the preacher's tongue, the author's pen, or the layman's money, it is to be used in a far more significant cause than lopping off the ear of Malchus or the head of a Communist.

In John 18:37, Jesus says,

> "To this end was I born, and
> for this cause came I into the
> world, that I should bear
> witness unto the truth."

This statement explicitly expresses the purpose for which the church is in the world. This is not to imply that the Christian is to abdicate his social or political obligations, but that he is to major in witnessing to the truth.

> And if anyone's name was not
> found recorded in the book of
> life, he was thrown into
> the lake of fire.
> Revelation 20:15/*TLB*

YOUNG MAN, EVER CONSIDER SHORT TERM MISSIONARY WORK OVERSEAS?
AND WIND UP IN SOME CANNIBAL'S POT. NO THANKS! I'VE SEEN TOO MANY OF THOSE TARZAN MOVIES...
SPORTS

It is inconceivable
that the Head of the
Church would leave his
Body (the Church) on
earth with nothing to do.

12 What! Closed doors?

"Because you are living in a
world of closed and closing
mission fields, you will be wise
to get some thorough training
in a secular occupation. This
will enable you to get behind
'closed doors' as a
non-professional missionary.
If, for example, you train as
a secretary, you can work for
a commercial company overseas
and then serve the Lord after
hours and on weekends. The
same is true if you train to be
an engineer, a doctor, or
a lawyer, etc."

That's what the man said and he ought to
know—he was a preacher.

But let's take a close look at his statement.
Did Jesus anywhere suggest that his program
of world evangelism would be accomplished

by men and women who would "moonlight" for him? When he chose his disciples, was it his intent that they should continue in their occupation as fishermen and then serve him "on the side"? Or did they understand that they were to leave their nets and follow him?

When God separated Paul unto himself, was it with the intent that Paul should continue his tentmaking and then do what he could to preach the gospel in his spare time? Is it not clear in the book of Acts that the Apostles knew they were set aside by God to give their undivided attention to prayer and to the ministry of the Word?

You are doubtless aware that the world's largest corporation today is General Motors, Inc. How did this multimillion dollar organization become what it is? Did it grow to such proportions as a result of the employees of the Henry Ford Company moonlighting for General Motors? It is obvious that no corporation could become what General Motors has become, apart from the dedication of men who gave their time, ability, and energy to that end. It is inconceivable that an organization the size of GM could have become what it is through the efforts of spare-time workers.

It is nothing short of an insult to the administrative wisdom of the Holy Spirit to suggest that he is going to accomplish his program of world evangelism through the labors of "moonlighters." If world evangelism is to be completed (and it will), it must to a large extent be done through the lives of thousands of men and women who know they have been set aside by the Spirit of God for the specific purpose of proclaiming the Good News of God's love for people. They must be men and women who are committed to nothing less than full-time service. They must give undivided attention to the task of missions.

This is not to underestimate the importance of Christian laymen. Obviously, Christian work can no more be carried on today without the efforts of laymen than the Old Testament priests and Levites could carry on their work without the support of the laymen of Israel. Furthermore, the fact that there are "non-professional" missionaries around the world who faithfully carry on a responsible witness for Christ while being true to their secular responsibilities is well and good. Christian laymen overseas again and again encourage and supplement the work of the "professional" missionary. This is as it should be. And let it be gratefully acknowledged that in those countries where the "professional" missionary is not allowed entrance, Christian businessmen are sharing the gospel with the unsaved.

But what about this story of closed doors? Is it really as threatening as some would make it appear? The answer is easily discovered. A copy of the *North American Protestant Ministries Overseas* along with a good map of the world will give us the picture.

It is true that China, the most populous nation of the world has been closed to missions for a number of years. However, let's not forget that the gospel message has been getting into the country via radio. Some other countries that have been restrictive or into which it has been impossible for American missionaries to go are Cuba, Sudan, Angola, Mozambique, Guinea, Somalia, Iraq, and Syria.

Other countries, once difficult for Protestant missionaries to enter, are now relaxing their restrictions. They are Laos, Indonesia, Portugal, Spain, and Nepal.

It is noteworthy that North Americans make up 70 percent of the world's Protestant missionary staff. In the last twenty years their number has increased in every area of the world. Though the number of American Protestant missionaries in Asia is slightly lower today than it was five years ago, it is still higher than it was ten years ago.

On the continent of Africa there are a third again more missionaries today than a decade ago. Many of Africa's new countries are wide open to the preaching of the gospel. Of the forty-five republics found in the continent, not more than five or six are closed to the foreign missionary.

Perhaps no continent is more open to the preaching of the gospel today than South America. The number of Protestant missionaries in Latin America has more than doubled in the last ten years. It has now become the number one area of the world into which American Protestant missionaries are going. A new openness toward the gospel message and the work of the missionary is found on almost every hand.

The country of Brazil with approximately 100 million people ranks first in the number of foreign missionaries in South America. The church of Jesus Christ is growing faster in Brazil than the rate of population increase.

The number of American Protestant missionaries serving in Europe increased 400 percent between 1950 and 1965. In Oceania the increase was 500 percent.

Though government restrictions have cut the number of American missionaries in India to 1,517, there are still a large number of European missionaries in that Asian land. Japan has been wide open to the proclamation of the Christian message since the close of World War II. Though economic prosperity has contributed to the growing indifference of many Japanese toward the message of

Christ, the country itself is open to the foreign missionary.

The fact that many evangelical mission societies are calling for missionaries today clearly refutes any suggestion that we are living in a world of closed doors. In the 100 evangelical missionary societies (denominational and interdenominational) which are now calling for missionaries, there is a total of more than 7,000 openings.

We are not living in a world of closed doors in any broad sense of the word. Furthermore, we never will live under such conditions. This dogmatic statement grows out of a very significant scriptural truth. Jesus Christ is the Head of the Church. The Church is his Body. It is totally inconceivable that the Head would leave his Body on earth with nothing to do. As long as the Church is on earth, it will have a responsibility to fulfill. In one word, that responsibility is "missions." He who opens and closes the doors of nations will never allow all the doors to be closed while his Body is still on earth.

Or to use another scriptural analogy, Jesus Christ is the Bridegroom. His Church is the Bride. It is unthinkable that the Heavenly Bridegroom would leave the Bride on earth with nothing to do. The Church of Jesus Christ has never had more to do than it has right now. Furthermore, you may be perfectly assured that he who rules in the

kingdoms of men will keep the door open
for his work to be accomplished until it
is completed and until he returns for his
Church.

> For there is a wide open door
> for me to preach and teach here.
> So much is happening, but
> there are many enemies.
> 1 Corinthians 16:9/*TLB*

WOULD YOU LIKE TO WORK OVERSEAS ON A SHORT TERM BASIS?
IF THE MONEY'S RIGHT I'LL GO ANYWHERE

God is standing
in the wings
while the nations
of the world march
across the stage
of time.

What!
God is sovereign
in missions?

Does God ever attend beauty
contests? He did! And as a
result, Hadassah was chosen
to be the queen of a great
empire that stretched from
India to Ethiopia.

Does God ever become involved
in assassination plots? He was,
and the king of that same great
empire was saved from a
premature death. A whispered
conversation between Bigthan
and Teresh was "accidentally"
overheard. The king's life was
spared and the two would-be
assassins were strung up.

Does God ever get mixed up in politics? He did, at a banquet table with a king, a queen, and a prime minister. Dramatic results followed.

If you are knowledgeable of the Book, you know that I have taken these three incidents from Esther. Although the name of God is not mentioned in Esther, his hand is clearly seen, reaching deep into the machinery of human affairs and directing the course of history.

Though God is neither a capitalist nor a Communist, a democrat nor a republican, he is deliberately involved in the movements of nations. Those who look at the stage of history and fail to see God directing the action, miss the most meaningful aspect of it all.

The Bible clearly presents God as the Sovereign of sovereigns. He rules in the affairs of men. The nations of the world are as the small dust in the balance in his sight. The heart of the king is in his hands and he turns it any direction he desires. He raises up one man and puts down another. The Caesars and the Napoleons, past and present, rise and fall like the great waves of the ocean, unto whom God has said, "So far and no farther."

The Old Testament scene is one in which Israel is at the center of the stage. She is, at times, "divinely" victorious over the nations that surround her. At other times she is "divinely" defeated and scattered abroad. In all of this, the sovereign arm of the Lord of Hosts is plainly evident.

The repeated warnings of God's prophets are finally fulfilled in the bloody destruction of Jerusalem and the temple of the Lord—in spite of all God's promises and the pleading of his prophets; in spite of his interventions and revelations. Israel failed to accomplish the commission the God of Abraham, Isaac, and Jacob had given her.

The New Testament pictures for us a "holy nation," being gathered out from among the Gentiles. That nation is referred to as "the Church." As with Israel, so with the Church, God has given a task to be performed and directives to be obeyed. This is commonly referred to as "The Great Commission." And, indeed, it is great—great in its purpose, great in its power, and great in its proportions.

As God did everything possible to enable his people in the Old Testament to fulfill their responsibility, we have every right to expect him to do the same for the church. In fact, he has promised to empower the church to accomplish the task he has assigned her.

There have been increasing evidences in the last twenty-five years of the sovereign

hand of God opening and closing doors
for his church. On some occasions, that
Almighty Hand has seemed to gently grasp
the knob and open the door silently and
slowly. On other occasions, the door has
been violently torn from its hinges. And
in a few cases, the door has been closed.
Let me illustrate:

Europe

It was not until the close of World War
II that the church in America began to look
seriously at Europe as a mission field. In
the past two decades, a number of fine mission
organizations have enjoyed fruitful ministries
on the European continent. Child evangelism
and youth ministries are prospering in several
of the countries. Bible training schools have
been opened and churches are being planted.
House-to-house book sales and correspondence
courses are having an increasing outreach.
Even the doors of those European countries
for which missions held little hope ten years
ago are slowly but surely opening today.
Spain illustrates the point.

Africa

What shall we say about the great continent
of Africa? The conquest of Ethiopia by
the Italians and the ultimate deliverance
brought about by the Allied armies is an
old but exciting story. During the Italian
occupation, the number of believers

"multiplied greatly" in the midst of severe opposition. God's sovereignty shines like a beacon through the darkness of the Ethiopian story.

The Congo, too, is witness to the fact that God is able to bless and multiply his church even while "the heathen rage" and "the people imagine vain things against him." There are sections of the Congo today in which the church is experiencing unprecedented spiritual and numerical growth.

Less than ten years ago, some mission leaders were expressing fear about what would happen when various African nations gained their independence. In this brief ten-year period, over twenty such republics have come into existence. The majority of them have kept their doors open to the Christian message. In some of them the Bible is included in their school curriculum. Not a few of the rulers of Africa have a "mission school" background. In some cases these leaders have openly expressed their desire for the church of Jesus Christ to make a greater moral and religious contribution to the lives of their people.

Latin America

The picture in Latin America is optimistic. In spite of much student and labor unrest in many Latin American republics, the door has never been more widely open for evangelism than it is today. Fruitful city-wide campaigns are becoming almost routine in some of the countries. Bible sales are at an all-time high.

Missionaries who have ministered in Mexico for the last twenty years find present opportunities greater than ever before. Those who were serving in Colombia twenty years ago could never have believed that the things transpiring today would ever take place. The number of believers has increased 300 percent in the last two decades. The evangelical church in Brazil is growing faster than the population of the country. This is a time of unprecedented privilege in Latin America. There are even those who suggest that if things continue as they are now, South America will become a Protestant continent by the turn of the century.

Asia

As we look to Asia, we are particularly encouraged by what God is doing in Japan, Korea, Taiwan, and Indonesia. Before World War II, there was only a handful of evangelical missionaries struggling against enormous odds in the country of Japan. At the close of the war, Japan's famous sliding paper doors were opened and missionaries by the hundreds entered the Land of the Rising Sun. Today, fruitful church-planting programs and nationwide radio and literature ministries are prospering in that country. Never in the history of missions in Japan have her people had such an opportunity to accept the crucified and risen Savior of the world.

For the last twenty years, both the Taiwanese and Korean governments have been favorable toward the Christian message and the work of the missionary. Opportunities to plant the living Word of God in the lives of unsaved people could not be greater than they have been in those countries, and for this we must thank the Lord of Harvest. The protective umbrella of a pro-Christian government is not something to accept lightly.

It is, however, the nation of Indonesia that stands out most strikingly as an evidence of the sovereignty of God in granting to his church the privilege of preaching the gospel to a people without Christ. The failure of the well-planned Communist coup of October 1, 1965, has to be accounted for. What more realistic way is there to account for it than a recognition of the sovereignty of God? One has every right to suspect that if the Communist coup had been successful, the foreign missionary program in Indonesia would have come to an ugly end. But God had other plans. It is now estimated that a half-million Indonesians have made professions of faith in Christ in the last few years. There is a great hue and cry for missionary help in that land today.

The move of the Dalai Lama and 80,000 Tibetans from Tibet to India has exposed more Tibetans to the message of God's love than ever before. The amazing number of tribes to whom the gospel is now being given in their own languages is a heartening story. The vastly increased outreach of the Good News through literature and radio should encourage the heart of every Christian who is committed to the importance of the Great Commission. Even in "closed" countries, the gospel is being heard. Modern mass media have certainly made the entire world our parish.

But I am not "telling it as it is" if I forget the negative side of the picture. How does one fit the sovereignty of God and his desire for all men to hear the gospel into the framework of the world's largest nation? Why does God allow a bamboo curtain to keep 800,000,000 people in the dark? Is China to be forgotten? Is God not bigger than Mao Tse-tung?

Of course he is. But who can know the mind of God in this? It is not ours to question the purpose of God relative to what he is doing in China or as to what he will do through China. It is our job to pray for the Christians of China, to get as much of the Word of God into China as possible (via radio and literature), and to be prepared to enter China when God makes it possible.

In the meantime, the prayer of the early church will give us a proper perspective of world evangelism and the sovereignty of God whether we are facing crushing obstacles or overwhelming opportunities.

Then all the believers
united in this prayer:

"O Lord, Creator of heaven and
earth and of the sea and
everything in them—

"You spoke long ago by the
Holy Spirit through our ancestor
King David, your servant,
saying, 'Why do the heathen
rage against the Lord, and the
foolish nations plan their little
plots against Almighty God?
The kings of the earth unite to
fight against him, against the
anointed Son of God.'

"That is what is happening here
in this city today! For Herod
the king, and Pontius Pilate
the governor, and all the Romans
—as well as the people of
Israel—are united against Jesus,
your anointed Son, your
holy servant.

"They won't stop at anything
that you in your wise power
will let them do.

117

> "And now, O Lord, hear their threats, and grant to your servants great boldness in their preaching,

> "And send your healing power, and may miracles and wonders be done by the name of your holy servant Jesus" (Acts 4:24-30, *The Living Bible*).

This kind of praying enables one to see clearly the stage of world evangelism with God standing in the wings.

> I am the A and Z, the Beginning and the End, the First and Last. Revelation 22:13/*TLB*

The Great Commission
is not an option
to be discussed.
It is an order
to be obeyed.

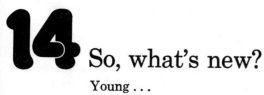

So, what's new?

Young . . .
Smart . . .
. . . that's our *now* world.
As swiftly and accurately as a
sidewinder tracking down an
enemy plane, the world has
raced toward that big day when
more than 50 percent of its
population would be under
twenty-one years of age. In many
countries, this is already an
exciting reality. This is a day
of young blood. Challenging new
horizons of privilege are all
around us, and young blood is

changing the complexion of the whole world scene.

How smart can we get? Through cool brain power we have made more technological advance in the last sixty years than man made in the previous sixty centuries. The universe of the microscope has been married to the universe of the telescope and we have landed in outer space. Facts, figures, and everything-else-that-goes-to-make-up-information doubles every ten years! Today's first grader will have more information thrown at him during the next eight years than today's college grad had during sixteen.

Highly-trained teachers, airy classrooms, TV lectures, cheap lunches, rented books, bulging libraries, well-equipped science labs, spacious gyms, football fields, strong fellows and pretty girls are all a part of our now world. Our modern high schools are better equipped today than our colleges were fifteen years ago.

College facilities are at one and the same time mushrooming and breaking out at the seams. Today we can live in wall-to-wall carpeted dorms, study in air-conditioned libraries, and major in everything from bobby pins to bulldozers. Our now world oozes with education. And we're just beginning!

"Affluent" is the word. Ours is a generation of sharper clothes, smarter styles, higher-powered cars, and gadget-filled homes. We eat more and travel far. We hear more, see more, and play more than any other generation. Ours is a money-saturated society where the man who wants it can get it for grabs. With the right breaks, he may become a millionaire at thirty. Sure, it takes a little work, but once he has made it, he only has to push buttons to get others to gather in more of the green stuff for him.

Wait a minute! Let's not get carried away. Some qualifications are in order. Our world is young, to be sure—and it is getting younger. Youth is on the march and is influencing education, economy, and government. But with all of the challenge there is in youthfulness, there are also hazards. Realism recognizes the tremendous contribution young blood is making to the progress of the world, but it does not close its eyes to the destruction that accompanies undisciplined uprisings, where irresponsible parents allow irresponsible youth to act irresponsibly. Nor is it blind to the fact that we have created a drug culture in which hippies take psychedelic trips to their own physical, moral, and mental destruction. Disrespect for law, rise in crime rates, crowded prisons, and overflowing mental hospitals all suggest that our *now* world is not as young, smart, and successful as it appears on the surface.

And who is responsible for this mess?

Obviously the generation that has given us the privilege of being young, smart, and prosperous is to blame—at least to a large degree. But we are responsible for what we do with both the technological benefits and the moral mess we find in our now world.

An astute Christian writer recently heard a young man say, "We have no respect for you; you have given us nothing to respect. But you won't admit it. You should be honest, realize that you are hypocrites, and stop going around parading with a self-righteous mask."

To this serious indictment the writer replied, "I agree with you. We are hypocrites, my generation. We strain at gnats and swallow camels. We fall short of the absolutes we try to pass on to you. We are a mess.

"But what hurts most is this: So are you. And I suspect that is why you are so bitter against me. You hate to see the mess perpetuated in yourself. You see your generation going down the same hypocritical path."

Nor are we so naive as to think that the whole world can be described as young, smart, and successful. Well over one billion people in our now world are neither young, smart, nor prosperous. What's more, the percentage of underprivileged is increasing every year.

Our world has a net population increase of more than 70,000,000 a year. The majority of these live and die in lands in which academic advance and economic success are limited to the few. While the shades of illiteracy keep the minds of millions shrouded with darkness, starvation stalks the lives of millions more who live on mere subsistence diets and go to bed hungry every night.

Let's be realistic. High-powered cars and four-lane highways, wall-to-wall carpeting and color television, three square meals a day and a college education—these are things enjoyed by less than a third of the world's people.

The thing our generation has to face in its now world is an answer to the question, "What can we do to change the picture?" Does the now Christian have an answer to the problems of the now world? Does Jesus Christ have a message for the space age? And what about his message for those who are still a far cry from the space age?

Because of the population of our world (almost four billion), we better start with a smaller unit. Let's start with the individual. That's where Jesus started. And after all, world population is just the sum total of its individuals.

The Bible claims and history demonstrates that the Christian message contains within it an explosive, transforming power. "New creature" is the biblical expression that explains the experience. It is an experience that has taken place in the lives of men and women of every generation since the day of Christ. It has encompassed individuals of every description; they run the gamut from stone-agers to twentieth-century teen-agers and from pagan cannibals to Phi Beta Kappas. The gospel of Jesus Christ has pierced economic, philosophical, political, and religious barriers and has influenced entire cultures for God. This is a bold claim, but with a bit of thought you can prove it to yourself.

Almost without exception, it has been the missionary movement that has brought cultural advance to the continents of the world. Literacy and literature, medicine and health programs, schools and education were completely unknown on most of the continents of the world in the premissionary era. It has been the ambassadors of Jesus Christ who have reduced languages to writing, printed textbooks, and established the educational systems in most of the once backward countries.

And who has done more for the sick and afflicted, the lepers and outcasts, for the widows and orphans of the world than the missionary? Medical clinics, hospitals, leprosariums, TB sanitariums, orphanages and retirement homes are the products of

the Christian message. They are the result
of the labors of men fired with a God-given
desire to serve their generation.

Nor has our now world outgrown its need
for such men and women. In fact, the need
was never greater. Our job of reaching men
with the gospel (and its fringe benefits)
is far from complete. The four billion people
who now populate the world and the six
billion who will be on earth by the turn
of the century present to the now Christian
his supreme challenge.

If the gospel is the answer for the individual,
then it inevitably is the answer for the
world. The problem is to win enough
individuals in any one area to accomplish
what will benefit all. It is with this in mind
that foreign mission societies have "help
wanted" signs out all over the place. They
are calling for thousands of missionaries—
two thousand a year for the next ten years.

The attractive thing about present-day
missionary opportunities is that they provide
an outreach for a great variety of workers.
Though there is no greater need than in
the realm of evangelism (be it personal
or mass), yet the declaration of the love
of God through other avenues is also
wonderfully possible.

There are mission hospitals that are either
standing empty or are operating at half-

capacity because of the lack of medical personnel. There is room for hundreds of doctors, nurses, lab technicians, and pharmacists in foreign countries. And how about the opportunities in literature, education, radio, and other media of service that are waiting for you?

Those who have what it takes to respond will be invited to invest their aptitudes, talents, and training as:

> Artists, musicians, printers, secretaries, accountants, agriculturists, translators, business administrators, doctors, nurses, lab technicians, educators, teachers, editors, camp directors, maintenance men, children's workers, youth workers, pastors or evangelists.

Our now world boldly challenges us with mission's greatest hour: greatest in conflicts and conquest, greatest in the number of missionaries, greatest in its number of martyrs, greatest in the expenditure of money, greatest in use of media, greatest in the response of nationals who carry on the program of missions, and greatest in its invitation to you to get involved.

Try telling God you are willing to get involved and see if he stops you. Perhaps a good place to start is in a summer ministry overseas. Hundreds of young people are doing effective jobs for God on foreign fields during the summer vacation. Why not be one of them?

Other young people are joining missionary organizations on a short-term basis. They go overseas for a year or two to fill specific needs. Because they are out there long enough to care, they often find themselves asking their mission boards for career appointments. If you are not sure of where and how you should invest your life for Christ then try the short-term approach. It may be just the thing God will use to give you the direction you need.

The supreme crisis in missions today is open doors. You don't have to seek job opportunities; they wait to be occupied. And if the now generation is to be reached for Christ, we must reach it. We must beware lest history record the fact that the sin of our generation was irresponsibility— the sin of unclaimed opportunities.

Ian Keith Falconer, missionary hero of another day, has something to say to us in this regard.

> "While vast continents are shrouded in almost utter darkness and hundreds of millions suffer the horrors of heathenism and Islam, the

> burden of proof lies upon you to show that the circumstances in which God has placed you are meant by him to keep you out of the foreign field."

The obvious need is for more committed Christians to take deliberate steps to move in the direction of our world's unmanned spiritual battlefields. Your response to Christ's invitation to follow him will lead you into a life of meaningful opportunities. And remember—his command to proclaim the Good News to all men is not a decision to be discussed; it is an order to be obeyed.

For I am not ashamed of this Good News about Christ. It is God's powerful method of bringing all who believe it to heaven. This message was preached first to the Jews alone, but now everyone is invited to come to God in this same way.

Romans 1:16/*TLB*

36-401